# The Best Day Ever

By Katy Forde

Illustrated by Nigel Buchanan

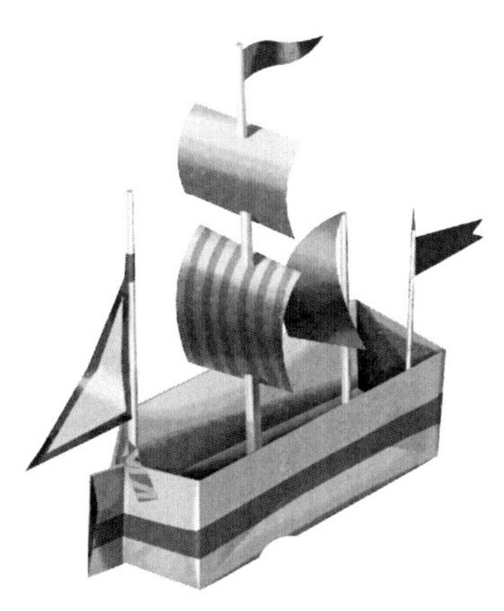

Pearson Australia
(a division of Pearson Australia Group Pty Ltd)
707 Collins Street, Melbourne, Victoria 3008
PO Box 23360, Melbourne, Victoria 8012
www.pearson.com.au


First published 2014 by Pearson Australia
2018 2017 2016
10 9 8 7 6 5 4 3 2



Publisher: Sabine Bolick
Project Managers: Tamara Pirois and Rachel Davis
Editor: Anne McKenna
Cover and series designer: Jenny Grigg
Designers: Jennifer Johnston and Nina Heryanto
Copyright & Pictures Editor: Julia Weaver
Mac Operator: Rob Curulli
Cover art: Nigel Buchanan
Illustrator: Nigel Buchanan
Printed in Australia by the SOS Print + Media Group

ISBN 978 1 4860 0731 8

Pearson Australia Group Pty Ltd ABN 40 004 245 943

Disclaimer
Some of the images used in *The Best Day Ever* might have associations with deceased Indigenous Australians. Please be aware that these images might cause sadness or distress in Aboriginal or Torres Strait Islander communities.

# Contents

Chapter 1

# The boy next door

A new family had moved in next door to Tye.

Through the fence, Tye could hear someone playing in the yard. It sounded like they were riding a skateboard or a bike, but Tye couldn't tell which. He scrambled to the top of the fence to get a better look.

A dark-haired boy was zigzagging over the lawn on a mountain bike. The boy looked up and skidded to a stop.

"Hello," said the boy next door.

"Hi," said Tye.

It was the beginning of the summer holidays, and from that moment on the two boys spent every day together. They rode their bikes, played computer games and found frogs in the local creek.

The boy's name was Masood, and he was from a country called Iran. At first, he could only speak a little English. But Tye quickly taught him all the important words, such as 'wheelie', 'tree house' and 'sausage roll'.

The holidays passed in a happy haze. It was hot and humid, so Tye and Masood sometimes played under the sprinkler.

"I wish the holidays would never end," said Masood, leaping into the spray.

"Me too," said Tye. "But at least we've got Australia Day to look forward to!"

"What's Australia Day?" Masood asked.

Tye blinked. “You’ve never heard of Australia Day?”

Masood hadn’t lived in Australia very long. “No, is it fun?” he asked.

Tye felt a hot rush of responsibility. This would be Masood’s first Australia Day.

“It’s going to be the best Australia Day ever,” he said to Masood.

Masood grinned, and did a cartwheel through the sprinkler.

Chapter 2

# Better than a barbecue

That night over dinner, Tye shared his plan with his dad.

"Guess what, Dad?" he said. "We're not having an Australia Day barbecue this year."

Dad scooped up some stir-fry with his chopsticks. "Hey? We always have a barbecue."

"Not this year!" said Tye, cheerfully. "This year, I want to do something special for Masood."

"Invite Masood to the barbecue," said Dad, chomping on a spring roll. "We chill out at the park, the neighbours drop by ... it's great!"

"But this will be Masood's first Australia Day!" Tye exclaimed. "It has to be better than a barbecue! Everybody has barbecues!"

Dad shrugged. "Sorry, mate. We're having a barbecue," he said.

Tye didn't reply. He was certain he could get Dad to change his mind.

After dinner, Tye sat down at the computer and searched for 'Australia Day'. His eyes flicked over the results. There were multicultural festivals, Aboriginal and Torres Strait Islander ceremonies, thong-throwing contests and meat-pie-eating competitions – to name just a few. Then Tye came across this web page:

This was perfect! Tye pictured himself and Masood watching the majestic yachts sail past. When Masood was eighty, he'd say: "That was the best Australia Day ever!" Tye ran to tell Dad.

"But we don't live anywhere near Sydney!" Dad exclaimed.

"That's what planes are for," said Tye.

"And who'll pay for the tickets?" asked Dad.

"I will," said Tye. He glanced at his toes. "If you could just lend me your credit card ..."

Dad locked eyeballs with Tye. "We. Are. Having. A. Barbecue," he said.

When Dad spoke like that, the argument was over. Tye's shoulders dropped so low his fingers touched the ground. Dad said Tye looked like an ape and went back to cleaning out the fridge.

Chapter 3

# The regatta

Tye and Masood spent most mornings riding their bikes in the park across the road. But today, Tye didn't feel like riding. He sat down at the edge of the creek, and tossed a twig into the water.

"What's wrong?" asked Masood.

Tye told Masood about his failed plans for the regatta. "I just wanted you to have the best Australia Day ever," said Tye. "But Australia Day is in a week's time, and I don't know what to do!"

The boys watched the twig float away.

"I know!" said Masood suddenly. "Why don't we have our own regatta? We can make boats and race them down the creek!"

Tye's eyes opened wide. He could see it all: a fleet of tiny boats, a cheering crowd… maybe the local paper would even cover the event! Tye imagined the headline.

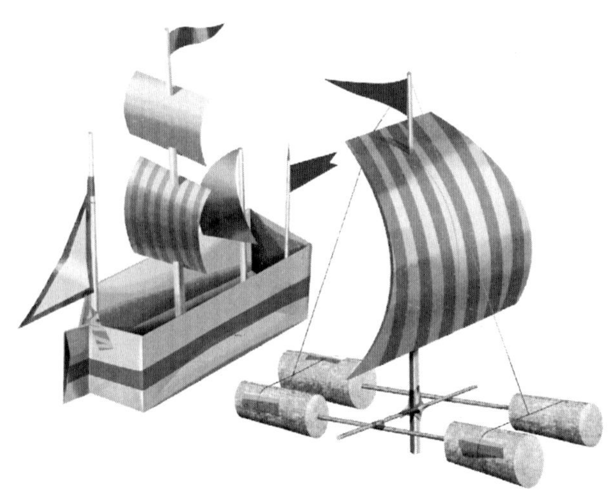

"Let's get to work!" said Tye.

So the boys made boats. They used anything they could find – milk cartons, chopsticks, corks. They decorated the boats with tall sails and tiny flags.

After five days of solid work, they had ten beautiful boats. With Australia Day only days away, it was time for a test run.

"Why do they have a regatta on Sydney Harbour?" asked Masood, as they headed for the creek, with the boats in a box.

"Because that's where the First Fleet dropped anchor," said Tye.

Masood didn't know the story of the First Fleet, so Tye explained how Britain had sent a fleet of ships to colonise Australia.

"Most of the passengers were convicts," said Tye. "They sailed across the world, and arrived here on 26 January, in 1788. That's why we have Australia Day on that day."

"And what about the Aboriginal people?" asked Masood, as they reached the creek. "How did they feel when all the ships sailed in?"

Tye gazed at the rippling surface of the water. "I don't know," he said, but his heart was suddenly heavy. He knew that terrible things had happened to Aboriginal people. He wondered what Australia Day might mean to the First Australians.

It was time for the test run. Tye reached into the box and pulled out a yacht. It had a sail of white envelopes, and a mast of chopsticks. Masood had even painted a little Australian flag on the sail.

"Please float," said Tye to the yacht.

Gently, carefully, he put it into the water. Immediately, it keeled over so low that its mast almost hit the water. The boys let out a cry. But then the yacht righted itself, and flew off down the creek.

It skimmed between rocks, then around the gentle bends and under the footbridge. Finally, it sailed out proudly into the pond at the end of the park.

Tye and Masood were surprised to hear cheering – a group of teenagers was watching from the footbridge. "Sweet!" yelled one boy.

Masood and Tye puffed up with pride. They quickly put all the boats into the water. What a sight it was as the boats raced downstream – it really was a regatta!

And that's when it all went horribly wrong.

One of the teenage boys had a big black dog, and its eyes were fixed on the boats. Suddenly, the dog twisted off its lead and plunged over the bridge into the creek.

The impact on the water sunk three boats, but the dog was just getting started. With a lolling grin, she bounded through the water towards one of the yachts, picked it up in her jaws and shook. Chopsticks and paper exploded left and right.

"NO!" yelled the boy on the bridge.

"STOP!" shouted Masood and Tye.

Masood, Tye and the teenage boy threw themselves into the shallow creek after the dog, but it was fast and slippery. With a leap, the dog was upon the flagship and snapped it in two with one bite.

It was an age before the dog was back on the lead. By then it had eaten six of the ten boats. The boy was so sorry that Tye and Masood found themselves comforting him, rather than the other way around.

"These things happen," said Masood.

But in their hearts, they knew the truth. With only two sleeps until Australia Day, there was no time to make more boats. Their dreams of a regatta were over.

Chapter 4

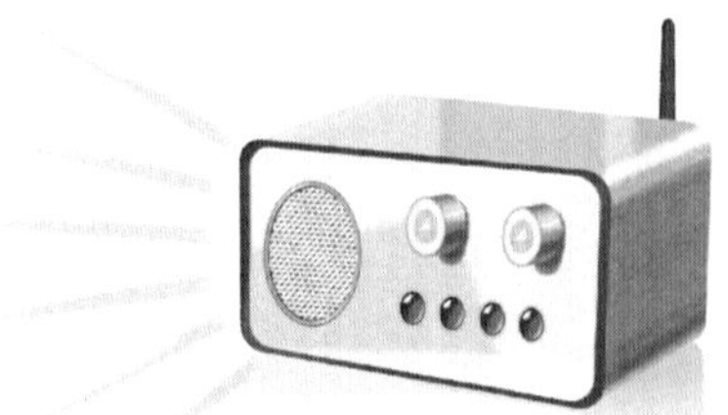

# The waterslide

The next day, the two boys lay on the floor of Tye's bedroom. They were listening to the radio and feeling depressed.

Then, the radio announcer said, "Australia Day is tomorrow, so I know you'll have big plans."

"Oh, rub it in," muttered Tye.

The radio announcer went on: "I know what I'll be doing. I'll be making a backyard waterslide. Australia Day is not complete without a slip and a slide."

Tye sat up slowly. "A waterslide," he whispered. "A backyard waterslide!"

Masood demanded more information. Tye quickly found video clips on the Internet of homemade waterslides. Masood watched in wonder as people slid belly-first along a long strip of wet plastic on the grass.

"We'll make a slide!" said Tye. "We'll film it, put it online and get a million hits! This will be the best Australia Day ever!"

The boys knew they needed help, so they headed immediately for Liu's house. Liu was an 18-year-old student from China. She was always making great things. Tye and Masood especially loved the robot panda with moving eyes that sat on the roof, and watched people passing by.

Masood rang the doorbell. The door flew open, and Liu's eyes scanned their faces.

"You've got an idea," she said. "I like it when people have ideas."

Half an hour later, Liu had found black plastic and two sprinklers in the "laboratory" (her backyard shed). The boys helped her spread the plastic out on the grass. It stretched all the way to the end of Liu's garden.

"We're going to be Internet sensations!" breathed Tye.

Liu gave the boys the job of adding foam to the border of the plastic.

"Is Australia Day your favourite celebration?" Masood asked Tye, while they worked.

"I don't know," said Tye. "Australia Day, Christmas, Easter, Halloween … they're all pretty cool!"

"We don't have any of those celebrations in Iran," said Masood.

"Oh," said Tye. He suddenly felt sorry for Masood.

Masood laughed. "It's OK! We have other celebrations!" he said. "Great ones!"

"Really?" said Tye, doubtfully.

"Our biggest celebration is Nowruz," said Masood, pronouncing the word 'no-rooz'. "It's twelve days long, and all the kids get money and presents."

Tye sat back on his heels. "That's funny," he said. "We have the twelve days of Christmas, and the kids get presents, too."

"We also have something called Haft-Sin," said Masood. "We paint eggs, and we put them on a table with seven things starting with S."

"We paint eggs for Easter!" said Tye.

"My favourite celebration happens on the eve of the last Wednesday of the year," Masood went on. "We call it 'Red Wednesday'. Everyone builds fires in the street and jumps over them."

"We don't have anything like that!" said Tye, his eyes round with awe. "Have you jumped over fire?"

"Of course!" said Masood. "Adults make sure it's safe."

"That's awesome," replied Tye.

"We also dress up as spirits, knock on neighbours' doors and get treats," said Masood.

"That sounds like Halloween!" exclaimed Tye. "We put on costumes, knock on doors and get lollies."

Liu hit a tent peg with a hammer. "In China, we have the Ghost Festival. People say the ghosts come out and look for souls to capture. We light fires on the side of the road, and burn fake money for the ghosts. We even put food out for them, but then we get to eat it!"

Tye was confused. “How can there be so many similarities?” he said. “China, Iran and Australia are so far apart.”

“All three celebrations are thousands of years old,” said Liu. “The answer is probably lost in time.”

Liu hammered in the last tent peg.

“Can we try it now?” asked the boys.

“I want to find something to secure the plastic first,” said Liu. “Won’t be long!”

Tye and Masood waited for Liu, their eyes fixed on the slide.

“We might as well give it a test run,” said Tye.

So they turned on the sprinklers at full blast. The water thudded onto the slide. The plastic shone like a fast car – sleek and inviting.

Tye touched the slide. “So slippery!” he murmured.

Masood ran a hand over the glossy plastic. “Smoooooth,” he whispered.

The two boys shared a cheeky look and launched themselves onto the slide. “Wooooooooo!” they yelled, as they shot down the slide like torpedoes. The wind whistled in their ears; the grass was a green blur at the edge of their vision.

They hollered so loudly that they didn't hear the 'rip, rip, rip' as the plastic tore away from the tent pegs behind them.

Later, after they'd begged Liu for forgiveness, they folded up the torn plastic. Then they wound up the sprinklers in silence.

Tomorrow was Australia Day.

Chapter 5

# Australia Day

The next morning, Masood was woken by a rapping on his window. It was Tye. Masood went outside in his pyjamas.

Tye looked excited and his hands were opening and closing like hungry bird beaks.

"We've still got time!" said Tye. "We can still make this the best Australia Day ever! We'll get some fireworks!"

"They're illegal," yawned Masood.

"OK, what about a flag-raising ceremony?"

"No flagpole," said Masood. "Or flag."

Tye fired off ideas. Hold an emu race? They didn't have any emus. Hire a famous Australian band? They had no money to pay them. Drive to the 'Australian of the Year' awards? They didn't have a car licence.

Suddenly, Tye sat down on the path and put his head on his knees.

"Epic fail!" he said. "Epic!"

Masood sat down beside him. "We'll have fun whatever we do."

"That's what you think," said Tye. "You're going to be bored out of your head. We'll have to settle for a barbecue after all."

Masood jumped up. "A barbecue?" he said. "We're going to have a barbecue?"

"Yeah ..." Tye said slowly.

Masood slapped his leg in excitement. "Ever since I arrived in Australia, I've seen them in parks, in backyards ... everywhere.

I'm dying to see how they work. We don't have them in Iran. This will be the best Australia Day ever!"

And it was.

All the neighbours brought plates of delicious food. Masood's family made kebabs, Liu brought Peking duck rolls, Tye's grandmother arrived with her famous Thai chicken, and Dad worked his sizzling magic on the barbecue. He even let Masood flip the prawns.

After the barbecue, Masood taught everyone the Iranian game 'Ghayem Bashak'. It was a bit like hide-and-seek, but when you were found, the 'seeker' called out "Sok Sok!" and you both raced back to the 'home' tree. If the seeker got to the tree first, you then became the seeker.

It was so much fun that they played it all afternoon.

And the following year.

And the year after that …